Joseph Buck Stratton

Hymns to the Holy Spirit

Joseph Buck Stratton

Hymns to the Holy Spirit

ISBN/EAN: 9783743418202

Manufactured in Europe, USA, Canada, Australia, Japa

Cover: Foto ©Lupo / pixelio.de

Manufactured and distributed by brebook publishing software (www.brebook.com)

Joseph Buck Stratton

Hymns to the Holy Spirit

HYMNS

TO

THE HOLY SPIRIT.

BY
JOSEPH B. STRATTON, D. D.,
NATCHEZ, MISS.

RICHMOND, VA.:
PRESBYTERIAN COMMITTEE OF PUBLICATION.
1893.

Copyright
by
JAMES K. HAZEN, *Secretary of Publication.*
1893.

Printed by
Whittet & Shepperson,
Richmond, Va.

NOTE.

THESE unpretending devotional effusions, which were published originally in the *Southwestern Presbyterian*, of New Orleans, are now, at the request of numerous friends, presented in the form of this little volume, in the hope that the reading of them may convey to some soul the spiritual benefit which the Author has found in the composing of them.

CONTENTS.

	PAGE.
NOTE,	5
INVOCATION,	9
THE OFFICES OF THE HOLY SPIRIT:	
THE LIFE-GIVER,	13
THE ENLIGHTENER,	15
THE INTERCESSOR,	17
THE COMFORTER,	19
THE WITNESS,	22
THE EARNEST,	25
THE REVEALER,	27
THE SWORD,	29
THE FRUIT OF THE HOLY SPIRIT:	
LOVE,	35
JOY,	37
PEACE,	40
LONG SUFFERING,	42
GENTLENESS,	44

	PAGE
GOODNESS,	46
FAITH,	48
MEEKNESS,	51
TEMPERANCE,	53

WORKS OF THE HOLY SPIRIT:

PENTECOST,	57
REGENERATION,	61
SANCTIFICATION,	64
ADOPTION,	67
COMMUNION,	70
UNITY,	73
LIBERTY,	76
THE INVITATION,	79
THE SPIRIT RESISTED,	82
PRAYING IN THE HOLY GHOST,	85
WALKING IN THE SPIRIT,	88
"LAUS SPIRITU SANCTO,"	91

INVOCATION.

SPIRIT OF TRUTH, within whose mystic cell
   Are gathered all things pure, and good, and fair,
   Who dost to mortals these thy jewels bear,
As ocean-caves yield pearls from cloistered shell ;
All that man needs to know 'tis thine to tell !
   Thy gifts with lowly suitors thou dost share,
   As the soft whisper of the intoning air
To voiceless wave gives chime of silver-bell.
Blind are our eyes till thou dost give them sight !
   Mute are our tongues till thou dost lend them speech !
Oh ! let thy quickening touch our souls,—incite
   To learn of thee,—and strive, with nobler reach
Of love and quest, to climb the sun-lit height
   Of the pure knowledge, thou dost deign to teach !

OFFICES

OF

THE HOLY SPIRIT.

HYMNS TO THE HOLY SPIRIT.

I.

THE LIFE-GIVER.

(Rom. viii. 11.)

ALL worlds, all beings, O thou Breath of God,
    Live through thine inspiration!
The stars of heaven, the sea, the flower-gemmed
        sod,
    Throb with thy vast pulsation!

Where thou art not—'tis death,—'tis nothingness!
    From thee come voice and motion;
As choral music, at the wind's caress,
    Springs from the depths of ocean.

Dead souls, that lie in palsied impotence,
    Revive at thy vocation!
They burst the tomb—they change their cere-
        ments
    To garments of salvation.

The sensual film drops from their blinded view;
    Life thrills with strange elation;
Old things are passed away—lo! all is new,
    As in a new creation!

Like wingéd forms, from the dark chrysalis
    To sunny realms translated,
O'er fields of Faith and springs of Heavenly bliss
    They range with zeal unsated!

O mighty Quickener, on me bestow
    This blessed resurrection!
And help me, by thy grace, to grow
    To Christ's complete perfection!

Oh! come, as morning air, o'er hill and plain,
    Comes to the earth's appealing!
Oh! come, till man's lost race shall live again,
    New-born, through thy blest healing!

II.

THE ENLIGHTENER.

(Eph. i. 8.)

FOR thee I long, O Fount of Light,
As one begirt with Arctic night
   Longs for the sun again;
To thee I lift my empty cup,
As thirsty plants to clouds look up,
   Crying for heaven's sweet rain!

Thy Word, I know, like starry skies,
Shines o'er me; but to my dim eyes
   There comes no cheering ray;
God's glory, e'en in Jesus' face,
My blinded orbs refuse to trace;
   My darkness knows no day!

Oh! purge my sight, that heavenly things,
Now veiled by earthly shadowings,
   May fill my clouded sphere!

And words of Christ, which now I note
With vacant mind, as barren rote,
    "Spirit and Life" appear!

Oh! spread thy brooding wing above
This inward void, as thou didst move
    Creation into birth!
Say to my soul, "Let there be light!"
Bid interposing clouds take flight,
    And heaven relumine earth!

Thine is the fulness,—mine the need!
In all the realms of life I read
    Thy boundless plenitude;
Renew, inspire, transform my heart,
Till, cleansed by thee in every part,
    God shall pronounce it "Good!"

III.

THE INTERCESSOR.

(Rom. viii. 26.)

OH! miracle of miracles!
    The Eternal Spirit stoops to share
My lowly wants, and gently tells
    My soul the thoughts it needs in prayer!

How like that sweet maternal art,
    Which in the callow bird excites
New force of limb—new strength of heart,
    To train it for its future flights!

How oft, dear Lord, when at thy gate
    I kneel, athirst to breathe my suit,
My faltering accents hesitate;
    My spirit sinks—my tongue grows mute!

The holiness which girds the throne
    At which I bow, my soul subdues

To awe-struck silence; and a groan
   Is all the speech I dare to use.

And must I then, as one debarred
   From mercy's door, turn sad away?
Wilt thou, O Father, thus discard
   The prayer I would, but cannot, say?

Oh! sweet response! An unseen hand
   Lifts from my heart its stifling weight!
A voice, than angel's note more bland,
   Cries, "See in me thine Advocate!"

"Speak out, poor child, thy timid tones
   I turn to language loud and clear!
I tune thy weak, discordant groans
   To music, God delights to hear!"

O Holy Ghost, thus, day by day,
   Enfold me with thy sponsor-grace;
That ever, where I kneel to pray,
   My soul may find God's dwelling-place!

IV.

THE COMFORTER.

(John xiv. 16.)

OH! glorious Trinity,
   A threefold life in thee
      In oneness lies.
As clouds in wreaths of gold
Within themselves are rolled,
Thy glory manifold
      Comes to our eyes.

The Father and the Son
And Spirit join in one,
      To save lost man!
In triple streams of love,
From the one Fount above,
Their blended currents move
      In God's great plan!

Not always o'er his sheep,
Doth Christ his wardship keep,
    At earthly post;
But e'er for their defense,
In loving recompense,
Sends to their orphan'd sense
    The Holy Ghost.

The promise infinite,
In scroll eternal writ,
    He so fulfilled!
Lo! from the upper spheres,
The Comforter appears,
Out of men's griefs and fears
    New hopes to build!

Thy voice I may not hear,
But thy co-equal Peer
    Speaks to me, Lord!
He doth my sight refine,
And make the things of thine
With light celestial shine,
    A living Word!

Thy presence, heavenly Guest,
Subdues my soul to rest,
    With memories sweet,
Of Jesus, and his grace!
Thy smiles reveal his face,—
Thy touch is his embrace,—
    Dear PARACLETE!

V.

THE WITNESS.

(Rom. viii. 16.)

O GOD the Spirit, can it be,
   That converse thou dost hold with me?
And bear'st in tones, by sense unheard,
But clearer far than spoken word,
The gracious message, "Thou art mine,
My child—my heir—by birth divine"?

Oh! keep that voice forever near,
To bless me with its notes of cheer!
For ofttimes doubts around me throng
In mocking troops, and turn my song
To choking sigh and anxious groan,
Lest thou my kinship should'st disown.

Or, the soul's torpor gives no sign
Of living light within its shrine;

Faith's quick'ning pulse is quenched in death;
From stifling airs I draw my breath;
My palsied tongue in prayer grows mute,
Like tuneless chord of unstrung lute.

Or if, in thought, I make review
Of work for God, so scant and few
My labors seem, that fear creeps in,
And clothes all life with taint of sin;
And conscience cries, in tone severe,
"There are no marks of sonship here."

Oh! softly, then, to my despair,
As waft of dove's wing through the air,
Is borne an answer on the breeze,
Joyous as angels' symphonies,
And soothing as Siloah's tide,
"Thou liv'st, poor soul, for Christ has died!"

"These sighs, these groans, this fierce unrest,
Are vital throbbings in thy breast!
This homesick eye, that skyward looks,
This thirst for heavenly water-brooks,

Do not these filial yearnings prove
The drawings of the Father's love?

" The need that seeks, like wearied bird,
An altar-nest in Jesus' word;
The prayer that says, with fire aglow,
' Dear Lord, I cannot let thee go';
Do these not show the mystery
Of wedded life 'twixt Christ and thee?

" Oh! weak disciple, burdened o'er
With conscious wound and bruise and sore,
Look up! thy Master and thy Friend,
His pitying glance doth o'er thee bend,
And woos thee to his arms to flee,
With the sweet question, ' Lov'st thou Me?'"

Oh! heavenly Witness, let my ear,
By thee attuned, be quick to hear
Thy blest monition's cheering strain
Sweetening earth's dirge with its refrain,
Till safe with Christ—my doubtings o'er,
I need thy solace—nevermore!

VI.

THE EARNEST.

(2 Cor. i. 22.)

I WALK the earth, an heir
   Of a realm beyond the sky,
Though now, I know not where,
   Its imperial regions lie;
But sure I am, the day will come
When its bright halls shall be my home.

I know in heaven my name
   With the royal seed is writ,
And Christ will own my claim
   With the princely throng to sit;
Who, faithful here the Cross to bear,
With him enthroned, the Crown shall wear.

It is but scanty fare,
   And the pilgrim's toil I meet,
In this hard world of care,
   Where I draw my weary feet;

But ever, as I march along,
I catch the coronation song.

Within my spirit's shrine,
   As an earnest of its bliss,
I feel the pulse divine
   Of a nobler life than this :
As eaglet in its eyrie pent
Forecasts its sunny element.

For thou, dear Lord, the seal
   Which my lineage doth attest,
Dost often to my sense reveal,
   In these yearnings in my breast,
Which tell that I, a child of sin,
Am now, new-born, to God akin.

Since thou hast deigned to be
   Of my lowly soul the guest,
In this blest unity,
   I can fold my heart to rest.
O Holy Ghost, thou pledgest me
That I shall share Christ's Royalty !

VII.

THE REVEALER.

(1 Cor. ii. 10.)

I CLIMB the mountain's height,
I soar on wings of light,
  In quest of thee, my God!
I search creation's maze,
Seeking, with tireless gaze,
  The way thy steps have trod!

But cold as shining star
In the dim depths afar,
  Nature thy form reveals;
No warmth the vision brings;
No loving answerings
  Respond to my appeals.

Not here—not here, my soul
Finds the supernal goal
  Its eager hopes pursue;

A God my spirit craves,
Who pities, loves, and saves,
   Holy, and just and true;

A Father, whose soft touch .
Gives strength to weakness, such
   As clasps the child about;
A Friend, whose patient care
Can all my burdens bear,
   And e'en my sins blot out.

To thee, O Holy Ghost,
Blest Comforter, who dost
   God's secret things survey,
To thee I lift my plea;
Do thou the mystery
   To my blind eye display!

Let Christ's dear image be
The link 'twixt God and me,
   Bringing the distant nigh!
Till in his sweet embrace,
I see him face to face,
   And "Abba, Father," cry.

VIII.

THE SWORD.

(Eph. vi. 17.)

O THOU who bear'st the olive branch,
    Who lay'st thy gentle interdict
On human strife, and lov'st to stanch
    The wounds which Wrong and Hate inflict!
Spirit of Grace! no murderous steel,
    Instinct with tiger's thirst for blood,
Gleams in thy hand!—For man's true weal,
    Thou wield'st thy sword—THE WORD OF GOD

Oh! blessed Sword, by Love enwreathed,
    By Truth with edge and point endued,
Ever in Mercy's cause unsheathed,
    Thou warrest for the sake of good!
Sin's bold entrenchments thou dost storm;
    Its fair devices thou dost pierce;
Where Satan walks in angel's form
    Thou stand'st, a foeman, strong and fierce.

As day-beam o'er the primal night,
   With flashing light and beauty broke,
Thou dost the realms of falsehood smite,
   And error dies beneath thy stroke.
The slumbering conscience feels thy thrust;
   Self-righteous pride falls at thy blow;
Nature's conceits thou turn'st to dust,
   As in the sun's shafts melts the snow.

Not Death's red spoil, O Holy Ghost,
   Thy kindly strategy would win;
Thou savest to the uttermost
   Those whom thy slay'st—by slaying sin.
'Tis when thy sword from reason's eye
   Cuts loose the films which mar its ken,
That souls, set free from sorcery,
   Awake to reason's life again.

Man sees himself through those keen rifts
   Which thou dost cleave through passion's veil;
And, freed from sensual fetters, lifts
   A wing that dares heaven's heights to scale.

The heart thou break'st, lets in the light
  Which shows in Christ a healing balm;
The reed, laid prostrate by thy blight,
  Springs from the dust,—a kingly palm.

With withered thigh and halting limb,
  Thou smit'st the bold, defiant soul,
That, chastened, it may lean on him
  Whose grace can make the wounded whole.
Thou prun'st the vine, that from its bough
  New shoots may spring—new clusters hang;
Thy power, that rends the bosom now,
  Unfolds new life from every pang.

Still wield thy sword, O Mighty Power,
  O'er regions now immersed in night!
Strike with thy blade, till strikes the hour
  That marks the reign of gospel light!
To preached word and printed page,
  Thy potent demonstration lend!
Wave o'er the fields where storm-clouds rage,
  And bid them into rainbows blend!

Still wield thy sword, O Loving Foe,
    Within this wayward soul of mine!
Its lawless hordes of lusts lay low,
    And change self-rule to rule of thine!
Purge with thy Word's incisive gleam
    Each lep'rous vice which lurks within,
Till in its light my features beam,
    Spotless as his—"who knew no sin!"

FRUIT

OF

THE HOLY SPIRIT.

(Gal. v. 22, 23.)

IX.

LOVE.

(Gal. v. 22.)

GIVER of life, no sterile root
    Thou plantest in the soul!
Thy heavenly germs to bud and fruit
    Mature, through Love's control.

Oh! if in me thy plastic power
    Has lodged the vital gift,
Bid Love to perfect leaf and flower,
    The sacred seedling lift!

Let Love to him who first loved me
    Quicken and warm my heart,
Till, like his own wide charity,
    In all life Love takes part!

Let pride and self-idolatry
    Be quenched within my mind!

And every thought and purpose be
   To Love's sweet sway consigned !

Let life, inspired by Christ-like Love,
   In Christ-like deeds abound,
A harvest such as saints above
   Gather on heavenly ground !

Giver of life, add grace to grace !
   Let Love to life be given,
That life on earth the way may trace
   To Love Divine in heaven !

X.

JOY.

(Gal. v. 22.)

NOT always drooping, like the bruised reed,
    Not always clad in mourner's sable weed,
Would'st thou, dear Lord, thy pilgrim people lead
      Through this life's wilderness ;
But oft, with sunlit face and rapturous song,
With hope exultant, and with courage strong,
Shouting hosannas, like the angelic throng,
      Thou bid'st them onward press.

As the dull mountain in the morning's flush
Gleams with a golden fringe, and the dead hush
Of night awakes to life's quick stir and rush,
      So when thy smile, O God,
Shines on the dreary realm within my breast,
Lo ! a new world, in Eden glories drest,
With joyous sunbeam gilding vale and crest,
      Spreads jubilant abroad !

My soul transfigured is!—The doubt, the dread,
Which secret sin and faithlessness had bred
Within my heart are gone! I lift my head
    And bathe in floods of light!
My gross perceptions, changed to visions clear,
In blythe excursions range the atmosphere,
Till heaven's bright domes and gates of pearl appear
    Almost like things of sight.

God's words of grace, in promise and decree,
Fall on my ear with living potency;
And Christ, in loving converse, says to me,
    "Rejoice, for thou art mine!"
Oh! then, there seems through heaven and earth to float,
In tuneful concord, from creation's throat,
The glad refrain—the universal note,
    "Rejoice, for Christ is thine!"

Spirit of Joy, the Primal Harmony,
Outbreathing Bliss of the Eternal Three,

Behold me groping 'neath night's canopy,
    And morn's sweet light bestow !
Oh ! grant, as erst thou dids't to Israel's seer,
That oft, from hill-tops midst these deserts drear,
Such Pisgah glimpses may my spirit cheer,
    While wandering here below !

XI.

PEACE.

(Gal. v. 22.)

THERE is a moaning in my breast,
    A plaint, as of the sea,
When battling winds break up its rest
    With their mad revelry.

On rolling waves each moment rocked,
    I rise—I sink—I seem
Like one by taunting spectres mocked,
    In some delirious dream.

My life's a shifting theatre,
    Where phantoms come and go;
My hopes are crossed, my footsteps err,
    My joys presage my woe.

The good I would I do not do;
    Discord prevails within;

Illusive things supplant the true,
   And lure me into sin.

Tossed to and fro in this wild whirl,
   To God my spirit flies;
And in his central rest, the pearl
   Of creature-rest descries.

O Peace of God! O Heavenly Ark!
   O Refuge of the weak!
Come floating o'er these billows dark,
   And bring the boon I seek!

O Holy Ghost! 'tis thine to bid
   These weary wrestlings cease,
And, in the Father's bosom hid,
   To give the soul true peace!

XII.

LONG-SUFFERING.

(Gal. v. 22.)

TO suffer—and to suffer long,
  With patient love, in face of wrong;
To strive to bless—and get no heed,
Oh! this is bitterness indeed!

To offer pearls with generous suit,
And see them trampled under foot;
To sow the wheat and reap the tare,
Oh! this is burden hard to bear!

To feel the sword, and yet invoke
Mercy on him who deals the stroke;
To plead with those who mock our plea,
Oh! this is keenest agony!

For other's good to pay the price
Of daily toil and sacrifice,

And yet be met with taunt and curse,
Oh! this is pang, than martyr's worse!

'Twas thus, O Christ, the crown of thorn
For us thy brow on earth has worn;
And still, though throned in heaven above,
Thou sufferest long for man's slow love!

O Holy Ghost! in me instill
The grace of Christ's long-suffering will,
That selfish greed and carnal pride
May on his cross be crucified!

Each day, from morn to eventide,
Do thou my march to victory guide,—
Till the dear Lord, at set of sun,
Shall o'er my trophies say, "Well done!"

XIII.

GENTLENESS.

(Gal. v. 22.)

OH! wondrous potency of gentle things!
    Oh! answer soft, that quenches wrath!
Oh! music, zephyr-born, of airy strings!
Oh! pity's tear! oh! love's kind whisperings!
    A might ye have no warrior hath.

The gentle snow-flake wraps the buried seed
    With fleecy shield from winter's death;
The gentle rain-drop slakes the desert's need;
The gentle sunbeam quickens vale and mead
    With flow'ry life and perfumed breath.

The whirlwind's uproar and the lightning's blaze,
    Confound and blind the inner sense;
The "still small voice," with tranquilizing phrase
Steals to the soul, and gently there conveys
    The words of God's omnipotence.

So Jesus scattered messages of grace
    On hearts with guilt and sorrow sore;
Lifting the downcast to his warm embrace,
By gentle speech re-uttered by his face,
    "I judge thee not!—Go, sin no more!"

So, not with fire from heaven would he consume
    The crowd who drove him from their gates;
So, not in wrath but tears, he tells the doom,—
Fraught with gaunt famine and the battle's boom,
    Which Judah's capital awaits.

So, not by force of martial sword and spear
    Would he his kingly crown maintain;
But through the truth,—beseeching men to hear,—
By love's attraction drawing rebels near,—
    He gently seeks the world to gain.

O Holy Spirit, Soul of Gentleness,
    This Christ-like mind in me enshrine!
The bigot's wrath, the zealot's fire, repress!
Let my ambition be—a zeal to bless,
    A passion pure, dear Lord, as thine!

XIV.

GOODNESS.

(Gal. v. 22.)

OH! in this world of woe,
    With sin's dark trophies strewed,
How passing sweet it is to know
    That thou, O God, art good!

Like heaven's pure air outspread
    O'er deserts parched and bare,
Thy wide compassions gently shed
    Their solace everywhere.

Thou mak'st the bright more bright;
    Thou still'st the mourner's sigh;
Thou show'st to sorrow's tear-dimmed sight
    Hope's rainbow in the sky.

'Twas thus the Son of God
    In goodness walked with men;

Flowers smiled along the path he trod,
  And Eden bloomed again.

His wealth was in his loss;
  His good was good to give;
His joy was joy to bear the cross;
  He died that man might live.

O Heavenly Dove! on me
  Christ's holy chrism confer,
That I may walk thus lovingly,
  His lowly follower!

XV.

FAITH.

(Gal. v. 22.)

OH! mystery of Faith, how like creation
    Thy wondrous transformations are!
Thou mak'st of empty space the habitation
    Of shining ranks of star on star!

Without thy light, the soul, with its high vision,
    Formed to traverse the realms of God,
Ignobly stoops from altitudes elysian
    To crawl, the tenant of a clod.

Oh! victory of Faith, there are no regions
    Whose walls thy prowess has not scaled!
From nature's depths to heavenly heights, thy legions
    O'er vanquished empires have prevailed!

Thou lead'st the trembling soul to Sinai's mountain,
  Where thunders God's condemning law!
Thou guid'st the penitent to Calvary's fountain,
  And bid'st him life from Jesus draw!

Inspired by thee, the simple wit of mortals
  The assaults of hellish craft defeats!
Convoyed by thee, they tread, through death's dark portals,
  The way that leads to angels' seats!

Girt with thy panoply, with port defiant,
  They face unawed the mightiest foe;
The stripling's rustic arms o'ermatch the giant,
  And lay his haughty boastings low.

Spirit of God! whose grace in bloody ages,
  The saints through martyr fires has borne,
Whene'er for periled truth the combat rages,
  Grant me the mantle they have worn!

My timid heart with hero's fire embolden,
  My sling with might celestial gird!
That I, by faith in Israel's God upholden,
  May battle do for Christ's pure Word!

XVI.

MEEKNESS.

(Gal. v. 23.)

THE lily, swaying to the breeze,
    Clad in its heaven-wrought draperies,
  And nestling in the sun,
Smiling on all who pass it by,
Whether with pleased or careless eye,—
  Outglories Solomon!

The lordly mien—the haughty brow,
The imperious will, that scorns to bow
  To voice of Right or Love;
The pride that others' worth disdains,
That recks not others' joys or pains,
  From me, O God, remove!

'Tis when, dear Lord, we learn from thee
The sense of our deformity,
  That grace self-love o'erpowers;

And, joined with thee in faith's embrace,
We catch the likeness of thy face,
   And make thy Meekness ours.

The living light thou dost infuse,
Like sunbeam flinging iris-hues
   O'er rugged crag or crumbling tower,
To nature gives new tint and form,
Till harshness grows to tempers warm
   In love's soft summer shower.

Oh! thou Inspirer of Christ's flock,
Convert to flesh my heart of rock!
   Purge it of sin's dark taints!
Gracious become, through grace bestowed,
Help me to tread the lowly road
   The Master showed his saints!

XVII.

TEMPERANCE.

(Gal. v. 23.)

TO use the world without abuse,
    Its joy to taste without excess,
Its gold to win, its dross refuse,
    Is heaven's strait way to happiness!

O Holy Ghost, whose wholesome touch
    Vice of its specious mask disarms,
Keep me from craving overmuch
    The witchery of pleasure's charms!

Repress those strong volcanic fires
    Which rage with baleful heat within!
Teach me to curb my wild desires,
    With self-restraint and fear of sin!

Help me, by faith, to fetter sense;
    To shun e'en good that leads to ill;

To quench the lust that breeds offence,
And chasten passion's prurient will !

In the sweet bondage of thy chain
    Let me walk forth, in spirit free,
From nature's loss extracting gain,
    From Temperance, Satiety !

WORKS

OF

THE HOLY SPIRIT.

XVIII.

PENTECOST.

(Acts ii. 1–5.)

LO! a sound like the wind rushing down
 through the air,
Smites the ears of a multitude gathered for
 prayer,
And a radiant shower, like the drifts from a
 cloud
Which the sunset has kindled, descends on the
 crowd.

'Tis the day Pentecostal—the day of the Lord!
When, with armor celestial, more potent than
 sword,
He has marshalled his legions, and o'er them un-
 furled
The imperial sign which should conquer the
 world!

Evermore should that sound, with the sweep of the breeze,
Bear the news of Redemption o'er mountain and seas!
Evermore, through the earth, in its breadth and its length,
Should its circuit increase and its voice grow in strength!

Evermore should the flame of that luminous sheet,
With its fiery tongues and its lightning-like heat,
Through the lapse of the ages, resplendent abroad,
Shed the life-giving sheen of the banner of God!

Evermore should the shafts from that quiver of light,
Pierce with meteor splendors the caverns of night;
Evermore should the Truth, in its jubilant march,
O'er the dark fields of error spread wider its arch!

Evermore! For the Crucified, raised to his throne,
All dominion and power has claimed for his own;
And the oath of the Father has sealed the decree,
"To the Son shall all kingdoms and tribes bow the knee!"

Yet, how slowly, dear Saviour, thy chariot-wheels roll!
How remote, through the battle's smoke, hovers the goal!
So entrenched are thy foes, and so fierce is their spite,
That thy people oft falter, and their hands cease to fight!

Come again, O thou Spirit of wind and of fire!
With a thousand-fold baptism Christ's armies inspire!
Give the church a new speech, and a heart all aflame,
To exalt 'mongst the nations Emmanuel's name!

Let the saints crowd again to the temple of prayer!
Let the arm of the Lord once again be made bare!
And his conquests go on till the welkin's broad dome
Shall resound with the pæan, "God's kingdom has come!"

XIX.

REGENERATION.

(John iii. 3.)

ALMIGHTY Spirit, at whose nod
    The obedient dust grew into man,
  Still thou dost guide the wondrous plan,
That makes of men the "sons of God."

Not will of flesh, not rite or cult,
    Can weave the sweet mysterious zone
    Which binds the sire and child in one;
Life ever is life's great result.

Each creature bears its special mark;
    A seed divine needs heavenly birth;
    God's offspring are not born of earth;
Stars are not kindled by the dark.

The breath which breathed o'er bleached bones—
   Lifts from their grave a living host,—
   Is thine alone, O Holy Ghost!
No mortal craft the secret owns.

From soil defiled and noisome cave
   The blackened ore thou dost extract,
   And purge with thy creative tact,
In melting fire or crystal wave.

So human souls, in death robes swathed,
   Thou bid'st their sepulchres forsake,
   And to a life celestial wake,
Like Naaman in the Jordan bathed.

From darkened eyes the scales are torn;
   Sin's baleful blight quits hand and heart;
   Foul spirits from the breast depart,
Like ghostly shapes at flush of morn.

Such rare, such blest nativity,
   Which man not makes, but makes anew,
   Angels with rapt amazement view,
And joy, Christ's travail thus to see.

My soul its blissful pulses knows,
    And knows them true; but ah! so faint
    That oft I breathe the impatient plaint,
"Send, Lord, not draughts, but overflows!"

Wider and wider spread abroad
    Thy quickening power, like flood and flame,
    Till earth, like heaven, through Jesus' name,
Shall peopled be with "sons of God!"

XX.

SANCTIFICATION.

(2 Thess. ii. 13.)

FROM heaven's pure realm, O Holy Dove,
   Thou com'st to men on silver wing,
   And evermore thy visits bring
Gleams from the world of light above!

As seed lies buried in the sod,
   Or wrapped inert in mummy's shroud,
   Till quickening touch of sun and cloud
Lifts it to life, a flower of God;

So human souls, from earthly mould,
   Breathed on by thee, in beauty rise,
   And catch from the o'erbending skies,
Their tints of azure, pearl and gold.

Thy work is, what thy nature is!
   Thou art, that thou may'st mortals make
   Pure like thyself, and bid them wake
From bruitish joys to angels' bliss!

Not lore of scribes,—not priestly spell,—
   Not chrism,—nor shrift,—nor sacrament,
   Can rear again the holy tent
Where God's Shekinah deigns to dwell.

We cannot scan the wondrous sleight,
   By which the Ethiop's cure is wrought;
   But sure we are, thy plastic thought
The visage dark can change to bright.

Somehow—the way we cannot guess,—
   On hearts which lift to thee their cry,
   Thou sheddest, as thou passest by,
Outpourings of thy holiness.

From forms and rites, to thee, the Soul
   Of life Divine, I turn my quest!
   I bare to thee my sin-stained breast,
And trust in thee to make me whole!

In leper's impotence I sit
    And loathe the chains I strive to rend;
    Be thou the link twixt means and end,
And raise me from the miry pit!

The bruised reed thou wilt not break;
    But aid it heavenward to aspire;
    So, nurse this germ of pure desire,
And from thy Fount its cravings slake!

XXI.

ADOPTION.

(Rom. viii. 15.)

OH! wondrous word, that tells the tale
 Of birthright lost and gained again!
 What heights of joy, what depths of pain,
To memory's view thou dost unveil!

The fatal lapse, the direful breach,
 That mark the fallen soul's decline,—
 That dim the star God made to shine,—
All thought, all measurement o'erreach.

The eye that mirrored heaven's own blue,
 By sin is bleared with tempers foul,
 Till alien look, and demon scowl,
Supplant the angel's native hue.

And yet from fall as deep as this,
   O Father, thou dost save thy child!
   And on the brow, by guilt defiled,
Dost print the sweet forgiving kiss!

And such thy love, that thou would'st have
   The fatling killed, the wine-cup flow,
   To let the wondering household know,
"This is a son,—no cowering slave!"

It is not the cold, grudging dole,
   The galling yoke, the mandate stern,
   Thou metest out, at his return,
But home-born cheer and joy of soul.

Oh! why, with eyes which cannot see,
   Will blinded scribes, who lead the blind,
   In servile fetters hold entwined
Those whom the Son of God makes free?

Ever, O Holy Ghost, I own
  Thy grace, which broke my bondman's thong,
  And taught my lips Faith's filial song,
"Whom Jesus saves, is God's dear son!"

XXII.

COMMUNION.

(2 Cor. xiii. 14.)

THE Grace of the Father, the Love of the Son,
   Commingling as streams which in confluence run,
Flow down from their sources in crystalline rills,
Wafting waters of life from the heavenly hills.

In sweet benediction, O Spirit divine,
Thou bearest these gifts, as the chalice of wine
To fever-parched lips bears the generous fruit
Conveyed from the vine through its cluster and root.

Thou cheerest my soul with the witnessing power
Of promise and pledge, as the spring-time's soft shower
Instils its warm life-blood in nature's chilled veins,
And mantles with verdure bleak winter's domains.

Thou sharest with mortals thy bountiful store,
As Christ fed the thousands on Galilee's shore;
Or stars, in the night-time, from infinite heights,
Divide with the ocean and lakelet their lights.

In fellowship tender, as friend holds with friend,
Thou makest thy strength with our feebleness blend;
To God thou dost lead us, and openest our ear
With loving accordance his counsels to hear.

Thou cleansest our thoughts, till, with lips undefiled,
Our prayer, without fear, we can lisp as a child;
Thou broad'nest self-love by thy genial constraints,
To charities wide as communion with saints.

Thou makest us feel in the household of God,
Like children reclaimed from their wanderings abroad,—
At home, where the converse has limitless range,
And heart answers heart in confiding exchange.

O Blessed Companion, Inspirer, and Guide,

Like wedlock's pure symbol,—the ring of the bride,
By sweet intertwinings, thy fingers of love
Embrace me e'en now, like the crowned ones above.

Be near me to chasten these natural ties,
When earthward would wander my over-fond eyes!
Be near me, to show me the Seal thou hast given,
Whene'er I forget my espousal to heaven!

XXIII.

UNITY.

(Eph. iv. 3.)

O SPIRIT, let thy music weave
    The strifes of earth to harmony!
Oh! lull their discords, as the eve
    Soothes into calm the troubled sea!

Thy Oneness is ineffable!
    For thou art God, and God is One!
And the wide thoughts that in thee swell
    Melt ever into unison.

Thou art not stillness, but a sound
    Which floats far as the zephyrs float;
But in thy strains no jar is found,
    For all are tuned to love's key-note.

Thou canst not be from self diverse,
    There are no rifts in thy sweet chords;

To several souls thou dost rehearse
   One faith, one creed, one chime of words.

Not thine the fault, O Voice divine!
   But ours the jaundiced mote and beam,
Which warp thy word's consistent line,
   And tinge thy rays with variant gleam.

Oh! why in human souls, wherein
   The love of Christ has been enshrined,
Should harsh distempers, born of sin,
   On battle-fields range mind with mind?

Oh! when wilt thou truth's radiant face
   Reveal so clear to our dull sight,
That in its orb no eye can trace
   A spot, a gap, to mar its light?

O Holy Spirit, o'er the eyes
   Of purblind men thy healing pour,
Till each 'neath other's garb descries
   The lineaments the Master bore!

Impress thy seal of unity
  On all who bear thine inward sign!
And show how kindly may agree
  The hostile clans of "Mine" and "Thine"!

Till, clasped as waves clasp on the strand,
  And fused, as mists at rise of sun,
The Church—no more a severed band,—
  At one with thee, shall blend as one!

XXIV.

LIBERTY.

(2 Cor. ii. 17.)

THOU takest captive, and thou makest free,
    Sweet Messenger of Grace!
In truest love thou bind'st the soul to thee,
    And other bonds dost thus displace!
Through thy wise sway, thou givest man the key
That opes the door to perfect Liberty!

There is no will to have the will supreme—
    No claim of lordly right to rule—
In hearts where thou dost dwell! The lawless dream
    Of pride is banished from thy school!
Thanks for the text, too seldom understood,
That lust uncurbed is fatal servitude!

The evil mind that has its own wild way,
    Unconscious makes the yoke it mocks;

In granite grooves its loosest movements play,
    Like rushing streamlet 'midst the rocks.
Discarding law, man finds himself has grown
To be the tyrant he would fain dethrone.

In thy pure channels, O Celestial Guide,
    My wayward passions kindly draw!
Control my will, till, like the ocean's tide,
    It bows its strength to Heaven's great law!
Thy fetters are my glory and my gain;
Beneath thy sceptre, I a monarch reign.

The soul that strives by its own thrift or pain
    To earn the meed of righteousness,
Is ever forging for itself a chain,
    Whose links, each hour, more closely press.
In bondage drear it plies its fruitless toils,—
Like him on whom the lifted rock recoils.

O Gentle Spirit, thou hast taught my eye
    To see in Christ the better way!
To him, with will subdued, I gladly fly,
    And on his strength my weakness stay!

I work no more in proud sufficiency,—
I work from love to him who ransomed me!

The worldling, groveling through these clouded days
   That span the space 'twixt birth and grave,
Walks trembling through a spectre-haunted maze,
   Through fear of death, a tortured slave.
I walk the earth,—whatever may betide,
In hope immortal, for my Lord has died!

Oh! more and more, help me, thou Holy Ghost,
   To clasp the bands of thy sweet thrall,
That more and more my joy, my crown, my boast,
   May be, that Jesus is my all in all!
In self-extinction, from false masters free,
Let me behold the life of Liberty!

XXV.

THE INVITATION.

(Rev. xxii. 17.)

IN a many-tongued speech, O thou Spirit of Love,
'Midst the clamor of life thy calm cadences move,
And with accent as soft as the sea-billow's foam,
When it touches the strand, whisper ceaselessly,
   Come!

Like the voice of a mother, they entwine their bland lay
With the child's cradle hymn, and seem gently to say,
"In the days of thy youth, ere the chill frosts benumb,
Oh! let sucklings and babes to the dear Saviour
   Come!"

With a voice which upbraids me with folly and fraud,—
With a treacherous heart that has wandered from God;
To the leper unclean, to the outcast from home,
Whose default calls for vengeance—they still utter, COME!

With a voice which floats in like a breath of perfume
To the mourner, revolving in silence and gloom
The dark tale of his woe, they transmute the sad tome,
To the legend of faith, "Lo! the Master has COME!"

With a voice that outvoices the thunders of law,
When stern conscience condemns me for crime and for flaw;
When, o'erwhelmed with my guilt, I sit hopeless and dumb,
They invite me to Jesus for pardon to COME!

With a voice which rings out like a trumpet tone, clear,
When the shadows grow dark and the death vale is near,
To the terror-struck soul they cry, " Fear not the tomb!
Thy warfare's accomplished,—thy Redemption has COME!"

With a voice which shall rise 'midst the roar of the shock,
Which the pillars of earth and of heaven shall rock,
They shall echo the Judge, as he counts up the sum
Of his chosen and faithful, and calls to them, "COME!"

Oh! thou sweetest of words! thou Evangel of Peace!
From the lure of strange voices my spirit release!
Let thy call go before me wherever I roam,
Till the pilgrim at last to his rest shall have "COME!"

XXVI.

THE SPIRIT RESISTED.

(Acts vii. 51.)

OH! direst frenzy of the soul!
   Oh! darkest record on the scroll
Of human sin! Oh! rage malign,
That dares to quench the fire divine
Of thy fond wooings, Heavenly Guest,
And drive thee, grieving, from the breast!

Shall panting hart refuse the draught
That to its lips the waters waft?
Shall parched field reject the rain
That comes to give it life again?
Shall famished babe with loathing turn
From the sweet fount of nature's urn?

Shall the imbruted prodigal
Reject the father's yearning call,

That bids him from his wanderings come
Back to the feast of childhood's home?
Shall man, with worse than swineherd's lust,
Spurn heavenly bread, to feed on dust?

O God! I tremble at the thought,
That I with this dread power am fraught,—
To lift this creature-will of mine
In conflict bold with will of thine,—
And bar the door, and cry, "Depart,"
When Christ stands knocking at my heart!

O God, that those by thee endued
With this high gift of angelhood,
Should use their gift, by deed or lips,
The Giver's glory to eclipse!
And, like the slave of demon's spell,
The evil choose, the good repel!

At this I marvel! But still more,
O God! I wonder and adore,
When o'er this scene of mad revolt,
I see the stroke of vengeance halt,

And hear thee plead with pitying cry,
"Oh! sinners, turn! why will ye die?"

O Holy Ghost! O gentleness
Of Love, which longs its foes to bless,
Teach these hard hearts, at last, to see
That Sin is malice aimed at thee!
Till the cold ice of unbelief
Shall melt at sight of thy strange grief!

And ever in this soul of mine,
Let thy soft hand, with touch benign,
Control each wayward wish and thought,
Till life in me, with thine inwrought,
Shall at thy bidding sweetly run,
As planets course around the sun!

XXVII.

"PRAYING IN THE HOLY GHOST."

(Jude 20.)

O THOU who dost thy banquets spread,
    And for thy guests the robe prepare,
On me, thy suppliant, kindly shed
        The grace of prayer!

Thy greatness, Lord, seals up my cry!
    Thy majesty rebukes my suit!
In voiceless impotence I lie
        Prone at thy foot!

So free thy call—so rich thy store,
    So keen the pangs which drive me near;
I still must linger round thy door,
        And crave thy cheer!

O Holy Ghost, whose pitying eye
    The starveling's timid haltings views,

Stretch forth thy hand ! the things supply
    I need to use !

For tinseled rag of Pharisee
    Clothe me with sackcloth's lowly grey !
While broken heart and bended knee
    My errand say !

With empty hand, outstretched to plead,
    Like Lazarus', for mercy's crumb,
Let me receive—not buy—heaven's bread,
    With tradesman's sum !

Let truth within my inward parts
    Each uttered phrase with meaning fill !
And spirit stir devotion's arts
    With vital thrill !

Give me the faith which in Christ's hands
    My guilt, my fears, my burdens lays ;
Assured the debt his Law demands,
    His Pity pays !

Give me the child's sweet confidence,
  That makes the parent's mind his own !
Whate'er I ask, be this my sense,
    " Thy will be done ! "

Let prayer to holy converse rise,—
  A union close with God above,—
An interflow of sympathies
    'Twixt those who love !

Oh ! ever thus, till that glad hour
  When I his face unveiled shall see,
Do thou, O Spirit, grant me power
    To pray in thee !

XXVIII.

"WALKING IN THE SPIRIT."

(Gal. v. 16.)

SHOW me thy way, O Heavenly Guide,—
    The way Christ's sheep have trod of old,
Lest my weak soul be lured aside
    From his safe fold!

The world without, the flesh within,
    Enclose me in their tortuous maze,
And veil the noisome walks of sin
    With beauty's haze.

Give me the eye, with vision clear,
    To note 'twixt true and false the line!
Grant me the ear that loves to hear
    The voice Divine!

Help me, by faith, to stand erect,
    With God's own pattern in accord,—

Conformed, not to man's code or sect,
    But his sure Word!

Cleanse thou my motive,—tone my will,—
    Make nature's spring-head pure and good,
That life may flow, in sea or rill,
    A limpid flood!

Not motionless, like passive clay,—
    Moulded and moved by priestly hand;
But free, as winds which know no stay
    On sea or land,—

Would I thy inspiration feel,—
    And walk as thou dost bid me go,—
As winged notes from harp-strings steal—
    At player's blow.

Draw me, each hour, with that constraint
    Which Christ upon his loved ones lays;
And by that sign, when zeal grows faint,
    My courage raise.

Give me the power to find in him,
    My peace—my strength—my righteousness;
As pulsing life from vine to limb,
        Bears its excess!

Teach me to yield my fond desires
    To thy pure sway—that, purged by thee,
Like incense breathed from altar-fires,
        Their flames may be!

Upborne by aspirations high,
    Above the lure of earth's decoys,
Oh! lead me on, with steadfast eye,
        To heaven's true joys!

But ah! in vain to that far height,
    My feeble pinion strives to spring;
O Holy Dove, aid thou my flight,
        With thy strong wing!

XXIX.

"LAUS SPIRITU SANCTO."

TO thee, O Holy Ghost,
   The universal host
      Of saints accord
Honor and majesty!
With voices like the sea,
They lift their songs to thee,—
      " Praise ye the Lord!"

For nothing less art thou
Than he upon whose brow
      Sits Deity!
Within that awful shrine,
Where dwells the Life divine,
Through work, and word, and sign,
      Thy form we see!

Thou wast at nature's birth
Inspiring soulless earth
    With God's own breath!
Thou wast the Witness when
The Lord came down to men,
To grant, through grace again,
    Release from death!

Through thy transforming leaven
Thou giv'st the health of heaven
    To sickened hearts!
The blind receive their sight!
The foul is cleansed to white!
The wrong grows into right,
    Through thy blest arts!

We magnify thy name!
Higher than the acclaim
    Of angels' choir
O'er Eden's sinless bloom,—
We hail thy dove-like plume,
Fanning in hearts of gloom
    Hope's sacred fire!

Oh ! come as erst thy wing
Came brightly hovering
   O'er Jordan's ford !
And bless the Gospel s flow,
Till all this world of woe
Shall Christ the Saviour know,
   And own him Lord !

www.ingramcontent.com/pod-product-compliance
Lightning Source LLC
Chambersburg PA
CBHW020258090426
42735CB00009B/1139